THE WORLD'S WACKIEST SPORTS STORIES

BY
MICHAEL J. PELLOWSKI

PICTURES BY
GREG HUCULAK AND ROSE-ANN TISSERAND

Published by Willowisp Press
401 E. Wilson Bridge Road, Worthington, Ohio 43085

Copyright © 1989 by Willowisp Press, Inc.

Printed in the United States of America

10 9 8 7 6 5 4 3 2 1

ISBN 0-87406-370-1

How did baseball player Jimmy Piersall celebrate his 100th home run?

What was the very special honor that Penn State fans prepared for Ohio State football coach Woody Hayes?

How did the greatest karate demonstration ever held really bring down the house?

What did a disgusted hockey fan throw on the ice when he just couldn't take the Los Angeles Kings' lousy playing any longer?

Find out about these and over a hundred other crazy but true sports tales in

THE WORLD'S
WACKIEST
SPORTS STORIES

CONTENTS

Diamond Dazzlers

Rib-Tickling Tennis

The Goofy Game of Golf

Bizarre Boxing

Who Said That?

Football Follies

Silly Soccer

Hockey Ha-Ha's

Basketball's Strange Bounces

Oddball Odds and Ends

DIAMOND DAZZLERS

Losing Is For The Birds

When it comes to pro baseball, losing is for the birds. That is exactly what happened at the beginning of the 1988 baseball season. The Baltimore Orioles started off their season with a record-breaking string of losses. The Orioles managed to lose their first 21 games in a row and established a new American League record.

Losing their first 21 games in a row was awful, but it could have been worse. The Birds fell 2 losses shy of tying the mark for the all-time worst start in baseball history. In 1961, the Philadelphia Phillies lost their first 23 games in a row. And there have been many other shaky starts in baseball over the years. In 1906, the Boston Red Sox lost their first 20 games. The old Philadelphia Athletics managed to equal that mark twice! The Athletics lost their first 20 games in 1916 and in 1943. Thank goodness winning really isn't every-thing!

A Family Affair

Sometimes brothers play on the same team. But in 1957, the old New York Giants baseball team had an unusual pitching combination on their roster.

When the Giants took on the Chicago Cubs on June 13 of that year, Jim Davis pitched the first 8 innings. He was yanked later from the game and replaced by his uncle, Marv Grissom. Grissom managed to secure the win for the Giants.

When asked about the game later, one of the Cub players remarked, "Maybe we didn't beat them, but at least we made them holler uncle."

Easy Out

Everyone knows big-league pitchers aren't expected to be good hitters. But who was the worst hitter of all? It could be Fred Gladding, who pitched for the Houston Astros from 1961 to 1973. Gladding was up 65 times and made only one hit during his entire career. Fred ended up with a measly .016 lifetime batting average.

Mound Miracle

Have you ever heard of a pitcher earning a mound victory without throwing a single pitch? It may seem impossible, but it actually happened to hurler Nick Altrock of the Chicago White Sox.

In 1906, the Sox were trailing an American League foe by 1 run in the ninth inning. Altrock came in to pitch for Chicago with the bases loaded and two men out. Before he threw a single pitch to a batter, Altrock picked a runner off first base to cause the third out.

Since Nick Altrock came into the game when Chicago was already losing, the pitcher before him was charged with the runs. Altrock couldn't be the losing pitcher, and he could only be the winning pitcher if Chicago somehow came back to notch the victory. And that's just what happened. The Sox scored 2 runs in the bottom of the ninth inning to win the game. Pitcher Nick Altrock earned a mound victory without ever pitching to a single batter.

The Long and the Short of It

Who were the tallest and the shortest major league baseball players? The tallest was 6-foot, 9-inch, John Gee, who played between 1939 and 1946. The shortest was the famous midget, Eddie Gaedel. Eddie, all 3 feet 7 inches of him, was signed by St. Louis Browns owner Bill Veeck to pinch hit. He went to the plate against the Tigers wearing number ⅛ in August 1951. Because his strike zone was so small, he walked on only 4 pitches. The pitcher couldn't throw a strike!

Romance At Home Plate

According to the law, there must be 2 witnesses at a wedding. When San Diego Padres traveling secretary John "Doc" Mattei decided to marry Jan Cantot in July 1980, the wedding ceremony attracted thousands of witnesses.

Doc Mattei and Jan Cantot were married at home plate in Jack Murphy stadium at the start of a game between the Padres and the Dodgers. As the band played "Here Comes the Bride," Jan strolled in from the left-field bull pen. She was joined at home plate by the groom, and the happy couple was pronounced husband and wife. Now that had to be the biggest wedding diamond in history!

Hey, Guys, Can I Play Too?

Shortstop is usually one of the busiest positions on the baseball field.

Toby Harrah set a fielding record in 1976, when he was a shortstop for the Texas Rangers of the American League. In a doubleheader (two games played back to back) on June 26, 1976, Toby played both games without ever touching the ball in the field. The shortstop had no putouts, no assists, and no chances to field the ball at all!

He'd Rather Walk

Jackie Jensen, a slugging outfielder for the Boston Red Sox during the 1950's, was afraid of airplanes. Jensen hated flying so much that he refused to travel to away games by air. He finally decided to retire from baseball rather than fly. However, he returned to the big leagues after a year of therapeutic hypnosis.

Dirty Player

Chicago White Sox player Minnie Minoso was very superstitious about his hitting. When he didn't hit the ball, Minoso felt that evil forces were working against him. Once after going 0 for 9 at the plate, Minnie ran into the locker room and jumped into the shower while he was still wearing his uniform! With a bar of soap, he began to lather himself. "I've got to wash these evil spirits out of my uniform," Minoso told his startled teammates. Minnie's weird shower did the trick. During the next game, Minoso smashed 3 hits!

This Could Get Boring

The Cincinnati Reds have been a major-league team longer than any other team. They used to be known as the Red Stockings. In 1869, the Red Stockings won 65 games and tied 1 game. They didn't lose a single game. The following year, they won another 28 straight games. Amazingly, the Red Stockings posted a record 94 games in a row without a single loss!

Beginner's Luck

In 1968, Mickey Lolich of the Detroit Tigers stepped up to bat in his very first World Series game. The Tigers were facing the National League Champions, the St. Louis Cardinals. No one expected too much from Lolich. After all, Mickey was the Detroit pitcher, and everyone knows that pitchers aren't good hitters. But no one told Mickey Lolich that pitchers aren't good hitters. The Detroit hurler swung and cracked a long home run. Mickey Lolich became the only pitcher in baseball history to hit a homer in his first World Series game.

Ouch!

In baseball, the idea is for the batter to hit the ball.

Steve Dembowski had another idea. He played second base for Fairleigh Dickinson University during the late 1970's. Steve attracted national attention for his work at home plate. But the attention Dembowski received wasn't for hitting the ball. It was for the ball hitting him.

Steve Dembowski was hit by pitches 36 times during his senior season in 1979. In all, Steve was pelted 112 times during his four-year college career.

Allow Me To Erupt

Baseball games are rained out sometimes. They have been snowed out, too. Once a game was even fogged out. But the strangest reason ever for postponing a baseball game due to weather was a volcanic eruption!

On May 21, 1980, a baseball game in the Pacific Coast League was canceled because of volcanic ash from the eruption of Mt. St. Helens. The ash in the air reduced the visibility at Spokane, Washington, and forced the postponement of a game between Spokane and Odgen. Well, you ashed for it!

Like Father, Like Son?

Mike Tresh taught his son Tom everything he knew about hitting a baseball. Maybe the son learned more than his dad knew. Mike played for the Chicago White Sox and the Cleveland Indians from 1938 to 1949. Mike's son later played for the New York Yankees. Tom hit more major league home runs in one game than his dad hit during his entire career!

Mike Tresh hit 2 home runs during a career that spanned over 1,000 games. Tom Tresh hit 3 home runs in 1 game on June 6, 1965.

Going Batty

John Wathan of the Kansas City Royals was rough on bats in 1980. Wathan once broke 5 bats in 4 games in July of 1980.

Expensive Souvenirs

Reggie Jackson was Paul Szafranski's favorite player. He really wanted a memento of Reggie. At a 1979 sports mementos auction in Tulsa, Oklahoma, would you believe that Szafranski bid $6,100 for a New York Yankees uniform shirt with number 44 on it— previously worn by Reggie!

Stop Bugging Me!

You've heard of baseball games being canceled because of rain, darkness, or even snow. In August of 1972, a minor league baseball game in Midland, Texas, had to be canceled. The game was canceled because of grasshoppers. Grasshoppers had invaded the stadium, and millions of them were jumping all around the playing field.

Run Happy

If a team scores more than 10 runs in a game, that's pretty good. Did you know that the Boston Red Sox set a major league baseball record by scoring 17 runs in 1 inning? It happened in a game against the old St. Louis Browns on June 18, 1953.

Time for Bed

The longest game in baseball history was played between the New York Mets and the San Francisco Giants on May 31, 1964. The game was held at Shea Stadium and lasted 7 hours and 23 minutes. After 23 innings of play, the exhausted Giants defeated the weary Mets by the score of 8–6.

Too Much of a Good Thing

Managers usually like left-handed batters to bat against right-handed pitchers. It was no surprise when Minnesota Twins manager Gene Mauch decided to use a left-handed pinch hitter against the Seattle Mariners' right-handed pitcher in a game in 1979. But sometimes you can overdo a good thing. Manager Mauch sent 7 left-handed hitters to the plate in a row. His team still lost the game 7–4.

The Twins' use of 7 pinch hitters in a row was one shy of the record. Would you believe that the Baltimore Orioles once used 8 pinch hitters in a row in a game in 1954?

Jimmy's Got It Backward

Outfielder Jimmy Piersall was one of baseball's zaniest players. When Piersall hit his 100th career home run he celebrated in a funny way. Jimmy circled the bases by running backward. Soon afterward, the major leagues outlawed backward base running on home runs.

Reverse Steal

When it comes to baseball's crazy characters, the king of them all is Germany Schaefer. Schaefer played for the Cubs, Tigers, Senators, and Indians from 1901 to 1918. As a member of the Washington Senators, Germany Schaefer pulled off one of the strangest steals in baseball history.

It all started when Clyde Milan of the Senators was on third base, and Schaefer was on first base. Germany wanted to draw a throw so Milan could run home. Germany stole second. But there was a slight problem. The opposing catcher didn't throw the ball to second. He just ignored Schaefer and let him get to the base safely. That made Germany mad. So on the next play, Germany Schaefer stole again. This time he stole back to first base. Schaefer ran from second to first trying to draw a throw. Soon afterward, a rule was passed that made reverse stealing illegal.

Older is Better

Who says major league baseball is a young man's game? In 1958, Ted Williams of the Boston Red Sox was 40 years old when he won the American League batting crown. Williams was the oldest player ever to take the title.

Addressee Unknown

In 1981, Steve Stone of the Baltimore Orioles received the Cy Young Award in the American League. The award is given to the league's best pitcher. When Steve received the plaque through the mail, he tore open the package. Whoops! The baseball brass threw him a curve. The award's inscription read, "Presented to Steve Carlton, Most Valuable Pitcher, National League." They had mailed him the wrong plaque!

Ka-Boom!

Talk about hits that light up the scoreboard! During a minor league game in Florida in 1984, a player hit a home run that smashed into the stadium's scoreboard. What's so strange about that? The hit caused the scoreboard to explode!

RIB-TICKLING TENNIS

Take It Easy, Your Highness

The sport of tennis is very old. It began in France over 600 years ago. The game of tennis has long been a favorite of the French nobility.

Because of its noble background, tennis is considered a polite and mannerly game. However, in the past it has also been a deadly game. Two French kings lost their lives because of the game of tennis.

In 1316, King Louis X played a tiring game of tennis with one of his servants. Right after the match, he collapsed suddenly. King Louis X died later, and it was all because he played an exhausting game of tennis.

In 1461, King Charles VII of France couldn't wait to see an important tennis match. In his excitement he rushed through his castle. He didn't watch where he was going and acciden-

tally bumped into a low beam. Even though he had a large bruise and a very bad headache he still went to the match. The French king never realized that he'd fractured his skull. Hours later he died from the injury. Now who says tennis isn't dangerous?

Whoops!

Sometimes tennis can be a very embarrassing sport. Just ask tennis pro Linda Siegel. Linda was an 18-year-old tennis star when she played in the Wimbledon Tennis Championships in 1979. Linda was matched against Billie Jean King, a very famous player. During the tennis match, Linda had an embarrassing accident. The strap of her tennis outfit slipped over her shoulder, and the top of her dress fell down. Whoops! To add insult to injury, Linda ended up losing the match.

John the Klutz

John McEnroe, one of tennis' greatest stars,
is known for his ability to swoop down from
nowhere and hit a great shot. At the 1980
Grand Prix Masters Tournament, McEnroe
became a falling star. During John's semifinal
match against Vitas Gerulaitis, McEnroe
charged the net to return a drop shot. John
got a piece of the ball but couldn't stop. He
tumbled backward over the net and knocked
over the net judge as he fell.

When he was a junior player in 1976, John
had an accident that was much worse than falling backward over the net. During one of his
matches he accidentally ran into a light pole
and knocked himself unconscious!

STUPID

THE ~~GOOFY~~ GAME OF GOLF

Now That's a Hazard

In golf the usual hazards are sand traps, patches of rough, and lakes and streams. The golf course at Hans Merensky Country Club in Phalaborwa, South Africa, has a very strange hazard—hippos! Ponds adjoin the seventeenth hole of the golf course with the Kruger National Park. In those ponds live families of hippos.

In 1987, the Phalaborwa Golf Classic Tournament was rudely interrupted by several wayward hippos. Golfers Jannie Ackerman and Paul Burley, along with their caddies, had to run for the trees when 2 huge hippos came crashing out of the bushes toward them. Luckily no one was hurt. After the runaway hazard hippos went back to their pond, the tournament continued. Now that's a golf hazard!

Pea Soup

The 1983 Inamoria Classic Tournament at
Torrey Pines Golf Course in La Jolla,
California, had to cancel its first round because
of bad weather. Was it rain, snow, or sleet? It
was none of those things. The round was called
off because of fog. The fog was so dense over
the course that the golfers couldn't see.

What a Splash!

In June of 1981, pro golfer Jerry Pate scored
his first victory in almost 3 years by winning
the Danny Thomas-Memphis Classic. How did
Pate celebrate the end of his golf dry spell? He
dived headfirst into the lake on the eighteenth
green with his clothes on! His victory celebra-
tion made quite a splash.

Ace in Lace

Rebecca Ann Chase of Dallas, Oregon, is
the youngest girl golfer ever to make a hole-in-
one. Rebecca was 8 years old when she made
her famous hole-in-one—called an ace. It came
on the 125-yard fifth hole of the Oak Knoll golf
course in Independence, Oregon, on August
15, 1977.

He's Getting Pretty Good at That One

Joe Vitullo, a retired golf pro, probably wishes he could play his whole round of golf on the 16th hole of a course in Hubbard, Ohio. In 1979, Joe sank a hole-in-one on the 130-yard hole. It was the tenth hole-in-one he had scored on the hole! He set the record for the most aces in one hole.

A Mere Babe

The youngest player—girl or boy—to ever score a hole-in-one was Tommy Moore of Hagerstown, Maryland. Tommy aced the 145-yard fourth hole at Woodbrier Golf Course in Martinsburg, West Virginia, on March 8, 1969. At the time of his hole-in-one, Tommy Moore was only 6 years and 1 month old.

What's Up Doc?

In 1962, Dr. Joseph O. Boydstone of
California established a golfing record by
hitting 11 holes-in-one in a single year. Now
that's an ace of aces!

That's Using Your Head

Golfer Mark Paliafito once used the head of
his mother, Geraldine Paliafito, to score a
hole-in-one. Mark was playing in a tournament
at Lac La Belle Country Club in Wisconsin.
His mother was a scorer. Geraldine was far in
front of Mark when he hit his tee shot on the
seventh hole. Mark's shot flew down the fair-
way and hit his mom on the head. The ball
bounced off Mrs. Paliafito and rolled into the
cup for a hole-in-one. Mark's mom was okay,
but she probably asked her son to go straight
for the hole next time!

Thank You, Operator

Norman Manley of California once collected a hole-in-one, thanks to a phone booth. Manley sliced a shot out of bounds. The ball hit a telephone booth and ricocheted back onto the green. It then rolled into the cup for an ace. We don't know if there was anyone in the phone booth.

BIZARRE BOXING

Quick KOs

Everyone knows Mike Tyson knocked out Michael Spinks in 91 seconds in their 1988 heavyweight title fight. Well, what took him so long?

On September 24, 1946, a crowd gathered at Lewiston, Maine, to watch a boxing match between 2 junior welterweights, Al Couture and Ralph Walton. However, anyone in the crowd who blinked an eye missed the entire fight!

At the opening bell, Couture dashed into Walton's corner. As Walton adjusted his mouthpiece, Couture threw a punch. Walton was knocked out instantly. The one-punch knockout ended the fight 10½ seconds after the opening bell.

A professional fight between Rob Roberts of Nigeria and Teddy Barker of England also

ended in record time. Barker and Roberts
were both welterweights. The fight was held in
Maestag, Wales. Barker decked Roberts at the
opening bell. He was awarded a technical
knockout when the referee stopped the bout
because a dazed Roberts looked unfit to continue. The whole fight lasted all of 10 seconds.

Another Kind of Boxing Ring

Pro boxers Willie Pep and Willie Pastrano
were superstitious fighters, and they both had
the same, strange good luck ritual. Before a
fight each one tied his wedding ring to one of
his shoelaces for good luck.

He Never Heard the Bell

Eugene Hairston was a unique boxer. Not
only was he a good fighter, but he was also
completely deaf. Hairston, a middleweight,
fought 63 fights from 1947 to 1952. He won 27
KOs, 21 as decisions, and lost 10. Only 5 of his
bouts ended in draws. Since Hairston couldn't
hear the bell, special red lights in the corners
of the ring blinked to signal him that a round
was over.

Turning the Tables

In June of 1980, Mustafa Hamsho won a middleweight fight in an unusual way. Hamsho knocked his opponent, Wilford Scypion, out of the ring with 40 seconds left in the tenth and final round. Scypion was knocked out of the ring and fell under the scorer's table at ringside. He could not get out from under the table and back into the ring in time to keep from being counted out.

FATTER THEY ARE

The Harder They Fall

The bigger they are, the harder they fall.
That is an old saying in boxing. In the case of
heavyweight fighter Ed Dunkhorst, that old
saying was true. Dunkhorst weighed in at 312
pounds for his bout against former heavyweight champ Bob Fitzsimmons in April of
1900. Fitzsimmons weighed in at a mere 172
pounds. Dunkhorst outweighed his opponent
by 140 pounds, but like the old saying says, it
didn't matter. Fitzsimmons knocked out
Dunkhorst in the second round of the fight.

All in a Day's Work

Andy Bowen and Jack Burke met in a
lightweight fight at the old Olympic Club in
New Orleans on April 6, 1893. In those days,
boxers fought until one of them was knocked
out or couldn't answer the bell. The Bowen-
Burke fight went 110 rounds and lasted 7
hours and 19 minutes. By round 111, both men
were too tired to continue. So the longest fight
in boxing history was declared a draw.

WHO SAID THAT?

Tattletale

In 1981, Al Cuccinello was a baseball scout for the New York Yankees. He was also the grandfather of a 5½-year-old boy named Mike. One day Mike asked what kind of job his grandpa had. Mike's mom told the youngster, "Grandpa watches other teams play, and then, tells the Yankees about it."

Little Mike nodded his head as if he understood. "Oh," said the youngster, "you mean he's a snitch."

Brain Teaser

Former NFL quarterback and coach Norm Van Brocklin had a witty answer ready when sportswriters asked him about the brain surgery he underwent in 1979.

Van Brocklin smiled and said, "It was a brain transplant. I got a sportswriter's brain so I could be sure that I got one that hadn't been used."

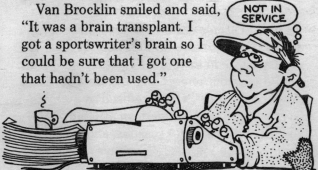

But What Was the President's Batting Average?

In the 1920's, reporters asked baseball star
Babe Ruth how he felt about making more
money than President Calvin Coolidge. The
Babe answered, "Well, I had a better year than
he did."

A Real Eye-Opener

Ed "Too Tall" Jones won fame on the football field as an All-Pro defensive end in the
1970's and 1980's. However, he took a year off
from football to try pro boxing. Jones quickly
returned to football after a tough year in the
ring. When asked about his year as a boxer,
Jones' friend and fellow defensive lineman,
Larry Cole, had this to say, "Yeah, Ed learned
how to keep his eyes open in boxing. He stays
awake more at team meetings now."

A Quitter Never Wins

Merlin Olsen's ninth-grade football coach
wanted Olsen to give up football. "What are
you trying to do to yourself?" he asked. "You
should use your energy somewhere else, like
the school paper." Olsen refused to quit. He
later became an All-American at Utah State,
an NFL All-Pro for 14 seasons, and a Hall of
Fame selection in 1982. Who says coaches
always know what they're talking about?

Let's Have A Look at That Radio, Jerry

Former U.S. President and college football player Gerald Ford once described himself as an avid baseball fan. He said, "I watch a lot of games on the radio."

Sports Squealer

In 1978, Lou Holtz was the football coach at the University of Arkansas. He was asked about the Arkansas Razorback football fans. "We have a problem with our fans, even though they're great," Holtz said. "When we are playing well, the fans cry, 'Woo pig, sooey, sooey.' When we are playing poorly, the fans yell, 'Woo pig, phooey, phooey!' "

It Doesn't Add Up

Talking about baseball, New York Yankee catcher and later Mets manager, Yogi Berra once said, "For 90 percent of this game, it's half mental."

Dollars and Sense

When asked about baseball superstar Richie Allen, sportscaster Harry Caray once said, "He's a million-dollar talent with a 10-cent brain."

FOOTBALL FOLLIES

Nice Spike

Football players like to celebrate scoring a touchdown by spiking the ball to the ground. Usually spiking the ball is a harmless way to show off. However, in an NFL game between the Kansas City Chiefs and the Pittsburgh Steelers in October of 1981, spiking the ball led to some real embarrassment for Steelers' wide receiver Dave Smith.

Here's what happened. Smith caught a pass and was headed for a sure Steeler touchdown. He was so excited that he decided to spike the ball. But he accidentally spiked the ball before he crossed the goal line! Smith spiked the ball on the 5-yard line. That made the spike a fumble. The wayward pigskin rolled out of the end

zone, and officials ruled it a touchback.
Instead of Pittsburgh getting 6 points, Kansas
City got the ball on their own 20-yard line.
And that's nothing to celebrate about, unless
you're a Chiefs fan.

Tape Measure

Football teams use lots of adhesive
tape. The Buffalo Bills of the AFC
use about 113,840 yards of tape in an
average year. In all, that's about
64 miles of the sticky stuff.
Wouldn't you hate to get stuck
with the bill for all that?

About that Touchdown, Jim...

The offensive players get to score the
points—and get all the glory. That's why Jim
Marshall, an All-Pro defensive end for the
Minnesota Vikings, was so excited. Like all
linemen, Marshall seldom, if ever, got his
hands on the pigskin. But in 1964, in a game
against the San Francisco 49ers, Marshall
lived the lineman's dream.

San Francisco quarterback George Mira
fired the ball to his halfback. The back was hit

immediately, and the ball popped free.
Marshall picked up the loose pigskin and
started running for the end zone. It was then
that Marshall's dream turned into a nightmare.
Jim was so excited that he ran the wrong
way—toward his own end zone! Marshall
streaked down the field and ignored the fran-
tic calls of his teammates. He ran 60 yards for
what he thought was a sure score. Unfortunately, instead of scoring a touchdown and 6
points for the Vikings, he scored a safety and 2
points for the opposing team, the 49ers. In the
end, though, Minnesota won the game by the
score of 27–22.

Running Wild

Quarterbacks in the National Football
League don't score many touchdowns.
However, on November 4, 1973, Chicago Bears
quarterback Bobby Douglass made NFL history by scoring 4 touchdowns against the
Green Bay Packers. What was even more
amazing was how many yards Douglass gained
while scoring those TDs. Bobby Douglass
gained all of 5 yards in scoring 4 TDs that day
in 1973. He had 3 touchdown runs of 1 year
each and another scoring drive that covered 2
whole yards.

A Fishy Story

We all have hobbies. Even football players have hobbies.

Defensive tackle Dave Stalls, who played for the Tampa Bay Buccaneers has 2 interesting hobbies. When he feels brave, he does shark research. When he doesn't feel brave, he goes bird-watching.

Car Crazy

Linebacker Jack Reynolds of the Los Angeles Rams has an unusual nickname. Reynolds is nicknamed Hacksaw. How did he get that odd nickname? When Jack was a senior at the University of Tennessee, he once spent a day and a half working on an old 1953 Chevy. He worked on the car with a hacksaw and actually sawed the whole car in half. That's how Hacksaw Reynolds got his nickname.

Super Stargazing

It's fun to try to pick the winners of NFL games. In 1979, 12 world-famous psychics met in order to predict the outcome of the Super Bowl game between the Dallas Cowboys and the Pittsburgh Steelers. What was their prediction? The star gazers said that the Cowboys would win by a slim margin. Maybe the psychics should just stick to telling people's fortunes. Pittsburgh won the 1979 Super Bowl, 35–31!

Passing and Failing

Today's football is a game of passing. So is going to high school. In New Jersey, there are 2 high schools that decided athletes had to pass their courses in school before they could pass on the football field.

These 2 high schools in the Newark District of New Jersey set a grade requirement for student athletes in 1983. The requirement stated that athletes had to maintain a *C* average to play sports. When football players at East Side High and Shabazz High School had their grades reviewed before their traditional

Thanksgiving Day football games, a problem
was discovered. Because of the academic
requirement, neither school had enough elig-
ible athletes to play. Thus, both of the schools'
traditional Thanksgiving Day football contests
were canceled. The days of the ignorant
athlete really are numbered.

His Favorite Receiver

Milt Plum came up with an interesting
offensive play in 1959. Milt was the quarterback for the Cleveland Browns in a game
against the old Chicago Cardinals. Plum
dropped back and fired a pass. The ball hit a
defensive player and bounced off his arm. The
pigskin ricocheted right back into the hands of
Milt Plum. So quarterback Milt Plum ended
up completing a pass to himself. Milt grabbed
the ball and ran for a gain of 20 yards. Some
people talk to themselves. On that occasion,
quarterback Milt Plum threw to himself!

Kooky Kick

Cortez High School took on Aztec High School in a football game on September 19, 1980. The two Colorado schools were evenly matched. When Cortez was held shy of a first down, Craig Ward was brought in to punt. His kick was quickly blocked.

The next time Craig Ward came in to punt, he tried to rush his kick. Unfortunately, he rushed it too much. Craig hooked the ball, and the pigskin sailed back up over his head. The crazy, backward punt sailed 38 yards in the wrong direction!

Crash Course

Everyone knows football is a dangerous
sport. It's a game where players can get hurt.
But have you ever heard of players hurting
each other before the game even began? It
happened in 1980.

Billy Waddy, a receiver for the Los Angeles
Rams, and D.D. Lewis, a linebacker for the
Dallas Cowboys, were warming up before the
game. Both players were on the field, catching
practice passes. They didn't watch where they
were running. CRASH! Waddy and Lewis
accidentally ran into each other. For several
minutes, they both lay stunned on the ground,
and the actual game was still 25 minutes away.
Luckily, neither one was injured seriously.
They both ended up playing in the game,
which Dallas won 34–13.

You Weren't Paying Attention, Blockhead!

It's always important to listen in the huddle.
Ron Drzemiecki played halfback for
Marquette University many years ago. Once,
in a game against the University of Cincinnati,
he came strutting back to the huddle after a
play. Drzewiecki looked at quarterback Dick
Shockey and bragged, "How did you like that
super block?"

"It was great," Shockey replied, "but you
were supposed to carry the ball on that play!"

Oh, Brother!

Football players run with the ball. Football
players also run in the Wistert family. The 3
Wistert brothers all won All-American honors
while attending the University of Michigan. All
3 brothers also played the same position.
Francis Wistert was an All-American tackle in
1933. His brother Albert was an All-American
tackle in 1942. And the youngest brother,
Alvin, earned All-American honors as a tackle
in 1947 and 1948. I guess you could call the
Wisterts an All-American family!

Super Bowl, Rose Bowl — Toilet Bowl?

When the Ohio State Buckeyes played the Penn State Nittany Lions in 1978, Buckeye head coach Woody Hayes was the target of a little bathroom humor. Nittany Lion fans handed out rolls of toilet tissue that had the face of Coach Hayes printed on the paper.

Official Foul-Up

Everybody was ready for the big football game between 2 rival high schools in New Jersey, on November 4, 1984. The game pitted the undefeated St. Peter's High Cardinals against their crosstown rivals, the Highland Park Owls. The teams, the coaches, the bands, and lots of fans from both teams showed up for the game in New Brunswick, New Jersey. But there was one little snag in the game plan. No football officials showed up. So the game had to be canceled, and everybody went home.

Thanks A Lot

Thanksgiving is supposed to be a peaceful holiday for giving thanks. That wasn't the case when the Miami Dolphins and the St. Louis Cardinals met in an NFL game on Thanksgiving Day in 1977. More than 50 Dolphin and Cardinal players got into a big brawl on the field. The players involved were fined a total of $14,000. It was one of the largest fines in NFL history. The coaches were just thankful that no one was hurt seriously in the fight.

Even the Scoreboard Was Tired

In 1916, football powerhouse Georgia Tech took on tiny Cumberland College in one of football's biggest mismatches. The game was played on October 7, 1916, at Grant Field in Atlanta. When the final gun sounded, the score was Georgia Tech 222 and Cumberland 0.

A Defensive Struggle?!?

The Oklahoma Sooners and the Colorado Buffaloes also put a few points on the board when they met for their gridiron contest on October 4, 1980. The final score of that game was Oklahoma 82, Colorado 42.

SILLY SOCCER

Won't This Game Ever End?

When Brighton High School and Gates-Chili High met in the semifinal game of the New York State Sectional in 1971, a soccer contest turned into a marathon.

The game began on November 2, 1971. At the end of regulation play and four 5-minute overtime periods, the score was deadlocked at 0–0. A winner had to be determined, but it was too dark for the players to continue playing that day.

The 2 schools continued the game on November 3. Gates-Chili High scored a goal, but Brighton managed to tie the score. After 4 scoreless overtime periods, the game was halted with the score knotted at 1 goal each.

On November 4, both teams took a break from their soccer game and met again on November 5. After Gates-Chili scored,

Brighton came back to score 2 goals. Brighton
won the game and advanced in the tournament. It took 3 days of play to decide a winner
in that unusual soccer contest. Now that's
marathon soccer!

Nice Kick, Keith

The N.Y. Cosmos and the Tampa Bay
Rowdies faced each other at Giants Stadium
in North American League Soccer action.
Tampa Bay forward Keith Bailey had the ball
with just under 30 minutes left to play. The
Cosmos were putting pressure on the
Rowdies, so Bailey decided to kick the ball
back to his own goalkeeper, Winston DuBose.
Bailey booted the ball with a strong kick, and
it sailed about 50 yards. DuBose couldn't reach
it, and the ball sailed into the net for a
Cosmos goal. Keith Bailey kicked the ball into
his own net and scored a goal for the opposing
team.

Follow the Bouncing Ball

Have you ever tried to keep a soccer ball in
the air for a few minutes, using just your feet,
legs, and head? It's not easy for most people.
But it's easy for Mikael Palmquist of Sweden.
In 1986, Mikael used his feet, legs, and head to
keep a soccer ball airborne for 14 hours and 14
minutes!

Growing Boys

When goalie William "Fatty" Foulke of
England stood in the net, he was hard to miss.
William was 6 feet 3 inches tall and weighed
311 pounds. Once Fatty arrived early for a
game and sat down at the table for the team
meal. Unfortunately, by the time the other
players arrived, there wasn't a crumb left!

However, Foulke isn't the biggest goalie
ever to have played soccer. That title belongs
to "Little" John Passler, who played for the
GH Metros in the American Cosmopolitan
League. Little John stood 6 feet 4 and weighed
in at 315 pounds when he came out of
retirement to play for the Metros in 1979.

Getting His Kicks

Roy Amundsen, an international soccer goalkeeper for Norway, sure got his kicks in a 1981 game in Oslo. Amundsen was kicked out of a game by referee Tor Moeien for pushing an opposing player. An angry Roy then pushed the referee to the ground and kicked him unconscious. Later the Norwegian Soccer Federation almost kicked Amundsen out of the league for his wild kicking spree.

Shoot-Out

In 1979, a man in Santander, Spain, fatally shot the soccer coach at his children's school. Why? Because the coach cut the man's children from the soccer team. No wonder good coaches are hard to find these days.

Just Plane Crazy

Many European soccer stars played in America's pro soccer league, the NASL (North American Soccer League), in 1979. Some of those players were unable to read or speak English. Player Karl-Heinz Granitza of West Germany was one such player. Granitza played for the NASL's Chicago Sting. Because he couldn't read English, the West German accidentally got on the wrong plane in Houston, Texas, in 1979. As the plane started to take off, Karl realized his teammates were not on the aircraft. He knew he'd boarded the wrong plane. He jumped up and started shouting in a foreign language. Everyone on board became alarmed. They thought Granitza was a hijacker.

Sorry, King, You Just Don't Understand

Would you believe that playing soccer was once against the law? Well, it was. In 1349, people in England liked soccer so much that they played it all the time. That really worried Edward III, the English king. He thought that the people were spending too much time on soccer and not enough time on archery practice. In those days archery was more than just a sport. Good archers meant a strong army. For that reason, Edward III outlawed the playing of soccer. However, the people paid no attention to the law and kept playing soccer.

A Goal for the Goalie

As everybody knows, goalies are supposed to keep the *other* team from scoring goals. Well, goalkeeper Jim Brown of the Washington Diplomats accomplished an NASL first on April 5, 1981. In a game against the Atlanta Chiefs in Atlanta, Brown made a save. He then picked up the ball and kicked it. The booming punt went the length of the field and ended up bouncing into the Atlanta net. It was the first time a goalkeeper had ever scored a goal in North American Soccer League play.

HOCKEY HA-HA'S

Machine-Gun Goals

When it comes to scoring goals in a single
game, no one yet has equaled the fantastic
feat of Quebec's Joe Malone. In the early days
of the NHL, Malone was a member of the
Quebec Bulldogs. In 1920, the Bulldogs con-
fronted the Toronto Maple Leafs in the
Stanley Cup play-offs.

In a game played on January 31 of that year,
Joe Malone alone scored more goals by him-
self than the entire Toronto squad scored.
Malone blasted a record 7 goals past the
Toronto goalie, and the Quebec Bulldogs won
the game, 10–6.

Bill Mosienko of the Chicago Black Hawks
holds the NHL record for the fastest 3 goals in
history. On March 23, 1952, Mosienko scored 3

goals in 21 seconds against the New York Rangers.

Dennis Potvin of the New York Islanders holds the record for the fastest 3 goals by an NHL defenseman. In 1979, Potvin tallied 3 goals against the Toronto Maple Leafs in 3 minutes and 21 seconds. That is almost a goal a minute!

Fowl Play

The NHL's Los Angeles Kings wear purple uniforms. In 1988, the Kings were suffering through a tough season. In March of that year, they were in last place and about to lose their 39th game of the year when a Kings fan decided he'd seen enough. The fan tossed a live chicken wearing a purple uniform out onto the ice during the Kings' losing effort against the Montreal Canadiens. What a fowl deed!

A Sick Story

The Stanley Cup is awarded annually to the team that wins the NHL Championship. However, in 1919, no Stanley Cup trophy was awarded. There were 2 teams playing for Lord Stanley's Cup, but neither got to take home the trophy. They went home with the flu instead.

Here's what happened. That year the Montreal Canadiens and the Seattle Mets were slotted for a face-off in the NHL Championship. The teams played 5 games. Montreal won 2 games. Seattle won 2 games. The other game ended in a tie. Before the series could be decided, a flu epidemic struck! Players on both teams became too sick to continue the series. And that's why a Stanley Cup champion was never crowned in 1919. The series was called off with the 2 teams tied.

When the Going Gets Tough, the Tough...

The Quebec Nordiques met the Boston
Bruins in an NHL clash in Quebec on
December 10, 1980. Quebec ended up losing
by the score of 6–4, but before the Nordiques
lost the game, they lost their goalie.

Nordiques goalie Michel Dion got angry
when the officials allowed an unassisted goal
by Bruins player Dick Redmond to count.
What did the angry Dion do? He skated to the
Quebec bench, threw his stick and glove down,
and walked out the exit door. Dion left the
game and didn't come back! The Nordiques
had to replace their angry teammate with their
backup goalie, Michel Plasse.

His Lifelong Goal

Did you ever wonder if hockey goalies are jealous of the other players who get to score all the goals? Ask Philadelphia Flyers goalie Ron Hextall. He got the chance to prove he could do more than just make saves. In 1987, Hextall became the first goalie in NHL history to shoot a puck into the opponent's net for a goal.

It happened in a game against the Boston Bruins. Late in the contest, Boston was losing 4–2. The Bruins took out their goaltender and put in an extra skater, hoping to score. That meant the Boston net was left unguarded.

Boston attacked the Philadelphia goal. The puck rolled free and went to Flyers goalie Ron Hextall. Hextall wanted to get rid of the puck quickly. He fired it high up into the air, and the puck came down on the ice and bounced toward the open Boston net. It skidded into

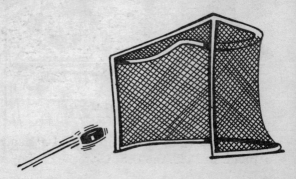

the goal before anyone could stop it. On that crazy, fluke play, Ron Hextall of the Flyers became the first NHL goalie ever to shoot a puck into the opponent's net.

But Could the Bus Skate?

Teams are always trading players. But in January of 1983, the Seattle Breakers of the Western Hockey League made a very unusual trade. Seattle traded the rights to player Tom Martin to the Victoria Cougars as a down payment for a bus that was owned by the Cougars.

Gold Medal Sub

An Olympic gold medal is a great achievement. In 1980, the U.S. Olympic hockey squad

earned first place honors, and Steve Janaszak
was a member of that winning team. However,
Steve Janaszak won a gold medal without
actually playing in any Olympic hockey game.
Steve was the backup goalie to Olympic hero
Jim Craig. Craig played every minute of every
game while Janaszak sat patiently on the
bench.

Scoring Goals is Tough — No Ifs, Ands, or . . .

Stan Mikita, the former star center for the
Chicago Black Hawks, was one of the greatest
players in NHL history. Mikita scored over
500 goals in his career. However, Stan's very
first NHL goal may be at the bottom of his list
of great goals.

Mikita was in a game against the New York

Rangers. Stan's teammate, the great Bobby
Hull, had the puck in the Rangers' end. Mikita
was parked near the Rangers' net with his
back to Hull. Bobby Hull fired a shot. The
puck hit Stan Mikita on the backside. It then
bounced off Mikita's seat and slipped past
Ranger goalie Gump Worsley for a Black
Hawk goal. Since Mikita was the last Black
Hawk to touch the puck, he got credit for the
score. It was the first and only goal the great
Stan Mikita ever scored by using the seat of
his pants instead of his stick.

In the Fog

Today's NHL hockey games are always
played on indoor rinks. That means games
should never be affected by weather, right?
Wrong! A game between the Boston Bruins
and the Detroit Red Wings at Boston Garden
on November 10, 1948, had to be postponed
because of bad weather.

After the teams played 9 minutes of hockey,
the game had to be stopped. No one could see
what was going on. A dense fog had settled on
the arena. The fog made it impossible to see,
and it also softened the ice. To prevent any
possible injuries, the game was postponed.

BASKETBALL'S STRANGE BOUNCES

Long Shots

There were only seconds left to play in the big college basketball game between Virginia Tech and Florida State in January of 1980. The two teams were deadlocked at 77 points each. Les Henson of Virginia pulled down a rebound just inside the baseline at Florida State's end of the court. He whirled around and fired the ball down the court just before the buzzer sounded to end the contest. Amazingly, the ball went into the basket to give Tech the upset win.

What's even more amazing is the length of Henson's long bomb. A full-size basketball court's floor is 94 feet long. From the baseline

to the basket is 4 feet. Les Henson's shot went 89 feet and 3 inches. It was the longest recorded shot ever made in basketball history.

High school player Barry Hutchings of Sutherlin High School in Oregon once made a pretty long shot of his own. Of course, his long bomb was second best to Les Henson's shot. Barry sank a shot 86 feet away from the basket in March of 1976.

Wake Up, The Game's Over

Pro basketball is one of the fastest sports around, thanks to the 24-second shot clock in the National Basketball Association. That means a team with the ball must take at least 1 shot before the time on the shot clock runs out. However, the NBA didn't always have a shot clock.

In 1950, an NBA team could hold the ball as long as it wanted before shooting. When the Detroit Pistons played the Minneapolis (now in Los Angeles) Lakers during the 1950 season, their strategy was to hold the ball as long as possible. The Lakers had 6 foot 10 inch superstar George Mikan, and the Pistons wanted to keep the ball away from him.

Every time Detroit got the ball, they dribbled and passed, and passed and dribbled. They never shot the ball unless they could make a sure basket. The result of the Detroit strategy was the lowest scoring game in NBA history. The Pistons won by the score of 19–18. It was also the most boring game in NBA history. Fans who paid to see the game were so angry that they demanded the NBA change its rules. The NBA did change its rules, and the shot clock was invented.

One-Woman Team

It takes team play to win a basketball game. All 5 players on the court have to work together. But what do you do when your whole team is made up of 1 player? Laura Merisalo had to solve that problem when she was a student at University Lake High School in Hartland, Wisconsin.

In 1978, University Lake played a school from Kenosha, Wisconsin. Unfortunately, more than half of University Lake's girls basketball team was sick with the flu. There were only 5 healthy players available for the game that day. One of those players was Laura Merisalo. Merisalo and 4 other players would have to play the entire game. University Lake had no substitutes on the bench.

Late in the game, University Lake was leading 25–16 when one of its players fouled out. Since they had no subs, University Lake continued to play with just 4 players. In the fourth period, another player fouled out leaving University Lake with just 3 players on the floor. Then there was more bad luck. One of the 3 remaining players sprained her ankle. That left just 2 players to defend a 33–25 University Lake lead.

But the game wasn't over yet. With 1 minute remaining in the contest, another University Lake player fouled out. Laura Merisalo was left all alone on the court—a one-woman basketball team. Believe it or not, University Lake still won the game.

Skunked

Shutouts are common in baseball, football, hockey, and soccer. But what about in basketball? One of the most lopsided basketball games in history occurred in 1918. It was a high school hoop contest between Shinnstony High School and Weirton High School in West Virginia. Shinnstony High shut out Weirton while scoring 136 points. The 136–0 win by Shinnstony is the widest shutout margin in high school basketball history!

Now, What Was It I Forgot?

When Coach Jack Gardner's University of Utah basketball team took on Brigham Young several years ago, first place in the conference was at stake. It was an exciting night for Coach Gardner and his team. Utah beat rival BYU by the score of 82–63. Jack Gardner was really happy. He ran around the court and congratulated all of his players. Then Coach Gardner jumped in his car and headed home. But in his excitement, he forgot something important. He left his wife behind at the gym!

Court Royalty

Wilt Chamberlain, who stands 7 feet tall and later became one of the greatest NBA stars, once scored 93 points in a single high school game. But did you know that he didn't come close to the all-time high school record for the most points scored in a game by a single player? The basketball superstar who holds the record, 156 points, is named Marie Boyd! She starred for Lonaconing High School in Maryland in 1924.

Number Please

When the New York Knicks played the New Jersey Nets in 1979, Knicks player Tom Barker ended up losing his shirt. Barker's uniform shirt never showed up at the game. When the New York coach put Tom in the contest, Barker had to wear a blank shirt with number 6 written on it in chalk.

The Old Switcheroo

In the 1978–79 season, the New Jersey Nets took on the Philadelphia 76ers in an NBA contest. Al Skinner and Eric Money played for the Nets in that game. Harvey Catchings played for the 76ers. Because of a protest, the game was suspended before it was over. The contest was scheduled to be continued at a later date in the season.

Before the game could be replayed, the Nets traded Skinner and Money to Philadelphia in exchange for Catchings and another player. When the teams finally got around to replaying the suspended game, Al Skinner, Eric Money, and Harvey Catchings had all swapped uniforms. Those players played in the same game for both teams.

Heads-Up Play

In 1955, two rival high schools in Minnesota took to the court for a big basketball game. The contest pitted St. Cloud Tech High School against Staples High School.

St. Cloud Tech player Tom McIntyre got a rebound. He looked downcourt and saw teammate Larry Nelson. But Nelson didn't see him. McIntyre fired a pass to Nelson, who wasn't watching. The ball hit Larry right on the head. It bounced off his noggin and sailed into the basket for 2 points!

Being a Referee is a Dog's Life

It's not easy to be a basketball referee. Once, official Bill Fouts was officiating a college game between Idaho and Gonzaga. The Gonzaga team had its mascot, a dog named Salty, on the court.

Throughout the game, the Gonzaga players and fans criticized Fouts' calls. Nobody on the

Gonzaga side seemed to like the job that
Fouts was doing. And that included Salty, the
Gonzaga mascot.

As Bill Fouts stood near the Gonzaga bench
and handed the ball over to an Idaho player,
Salty broke free of his leash. The dog ran over
to Bill and bit the referee on the leg.

After Salty was tied up and Fouts' wound
was treated, the game continued. And despite
Salty's continual barking, Idaho won!

ODDBALL ODDS AND ENDS

A Little Good-Bye Gift

Field hockey is a very popular sport in India and Pakistan. In January of 1982, a special field hockey benefit game was played to honor Pakistan's former field hockey captain, Islahuddin. Many worldwide field hockey stars played in the contest, which was held at Karachi. Fans who attended the game contributed to a fund for Islahuddin's retirement. It turned out to be quite a retirement gift. At the end of the game, Islahuddin was presented with the astounding amount of 2.5 million dollars!

Not Letter Perfect

Chet Gurick played football and baseball for Brooklyn College in 1943, and earned varsity letters in both sports. Unfortunately, he didn't get them right away. In fact, it wasn't until 36 years later that Gurick was awarded the letters that he earned earlier. In January of 1944, Chet left school and joined the Army. At a special Hall of Fame dinner in 1979, Chet Gurick was finally awarded his football and baseball letters from Brooklyn College.

Just Horsing Around

Jesse Owens could run faster and jump farther than anyone else in his day. At the 1936 Olympic games, Owens won 4 gold medals. His victory in the 100-yard dash earned him the title of the fastest man in the world.

In December of 1936, Jesse Owens ran a very unusual race. The fastest man in the world competed against a racehorse named Julio McCaw. The man vs. horse race was held at a track in Havana, Cuba, on December 27, 1936. It covered a distance of 100 yards. Speedy Owens was granted a 40-yard handicap advantage.

When the race started, Julio McCaw ran fast. But Jesse Owens ran faster and won the race, showing that 2 legs can be faster than 4 legs.

Don't Go in the Water

A racehorse can be scratched from a race for a variety of reasons. However, a South African racehorse named Quatrain was once scratched from a race for a very weird reason. Quatrain couldn't run in a race because she had been bitten by a shark.

Quatrain, a prize filly, was taking a day off from training. She was wading in the surf at a South African beach when a shark swam up and nipped her on the leg. Quatrain ran out of the water before the shark could strike again. To close the wound required 12 stitches, and Quatrain had to be scratched from racing for awhile.

Dark Days for the Lancers

The Rochester Lancers soccer team operated in the red in 1980. That caused the team to end up in the black.

Here's what happened. The local gas and electric company shut off the lights at Holleder Stadium, the Lancers' home field because they didn't pay their electric bill. Members of the team had to find their way around the dressing room by candlelight before and after a practice session. We don't know if they found it romantic!

Softball Marathon

In June 1986, 20 friends got together for a softball game in Los Alamos, New Mexico. They didn't stop until they had played 390 innings. It took exactly 100 hours!

Oh, My Aching Noodle

Marlow Gundmundsen of Lincoln Junior High School in Valia, California, found out that coaching track can be a real headache. In 1981, Gundmundsen was hit on the head by an 8-pound shot that was putted by an eighth-grade athlete. Luckily, Marlow ducked when he saw the wayward shot coming, or he might have been injured seriously.

Going Ape

Experts have been looking for a way to accurately predict the outcome of sporting events for years. In 1983, the Dallas Zoo came up with an idea that made the experts go ape. They let a gorilla named Kanda the Great try his hand at picking the winners of some National League football games. Believe it or not, Kanda did pretty well. He picked 9 winners correctly, and he was wrong only 4 times. See if you can do as well.

Slip-Up

Russian goalie Vladislav Tretiak was
considered the greatest hockey goalie of his
time in 1981. However, an unfortunate accident prevented Tratiak from playing in the
U.S.S.R. National Hockey Championships in
1981. Tretiak stepped off a bus near Moscow
and broke his leg. What happened? He slipped
on the ice, of course!

Tons of Ski Fun

In 1979, the world heavyweight ski
championships were held in Carrabasset
Valley, Maine. The winner of the contest was
John Truden, who took the title for the
third time. I guess you could say that
John truly qualified as a heavyweight
skier. Without equipment he tipped
the scales at 482 pounds!

Run For Your Life

A 15-mile road race in Kenya once took a strange turn. Marathon runners Chris Stewart of England, and Samson Kimowba of Kenya were at the front of the pack at the two mile pole. Suddenly, Kimowba started sprinting and raced past Stewart. "Where are you going so fast?" Chris yelled. "There are still 13 miles left to run!"

"Look behind you!" shouted Samson as he ran by.

Chris Stewart looked back and saw a shocking sight. A rhino had charged out of the brush and was chasing after the runners!

Pachyderm Pace

Horses race. Greyhound dogs race. Even turtles and frogs race. But the race held at Monticello Raceway in May of 1980, was like no other race ever held before. The race was a quarter-mile pace for racing elephants.

The contestants in that unusual race were 2 prize pachyderms named Nellie and Minny. Nellie weighed in at 3,600 pounds. Minny tipped the scales at a mere 3,000.

For some reason, the victor of the big race wasn't recorded. However, I'll bet she won by a trunk!

Taking a Short Cut

Grete Waitz of Norway won the New York Marathon several times. However, in 1981, Waitz had to drop out of the long-distance race because of injuries. After running 14 miles, Grete was in too much pain to continue. She stopped, borrowed some money from a volunteer at an aid station, and took a cab back to her hotel.

Itching to Get Out on the Ice

The U.S. Skating Team of Peter and Kitty Caruthers was favored to win the pairs competition of the Skate America Figure Skating Competition in Lake Placid in 1982. Unfortunately, they never got to compete. Kitty got the chicken pox, and the pair was scratched from the meet.

So What's New?

Are you angry because modern superstar athletes seem to be paid too much money? Relax. Famous athletes have been paid a lot of money for a long time.

Diocles, a famous chariot racer in ancient Rome, earned about 4,000 sesterces per day. Back then a shepherd earned about 80 sesterces per day. A camel driver earned 100 sesterces per day. And skilled workmen, like stone masons and carpenters, earned only about 200 sesterces per day. So you see, professional athletes have always been paid well.

Crash!!!

The greatest karate demonstration ever held took place in Bradford, England. It was also the wackiest demonstration. A Team of 15 karate experts showed up to do battle against a 150-year-old wooden house. After hours of karate chops and kicks, the house was demolished.

About the Author

MICHAEL J. PELLOWSKI was born January 24, 1949, in New Brunswick, New Jersey. He is a graduate of Rutgers, the State University of New Jersey, and has a degree in education. Before turning to writing he was a professional football player and then a high school teacher.

He is married to Judith Snyder Pellowski, his former high school sweetheart. They have four children, Morgan, Matthew, Melanie, and Martin. They also have two cats, Carrot and Spot, and a German Shepherd dog named Spike.

Michael is the author of more than seventy-five books for children. He is also the host and producer of two local TV shows seen on cable TV in his home state. His children's comedy show, "Fun Stop," was nominated as one of the best local cable TV children's shows in America.